STEM Projects in MINECRAFT™

The Unofficial Guide to
Building Bridges in
MINECRAFT™

RYAN NAGELHOUT

PowerKiDS
press

New York

Published in 2019 by The Rosen Publishing Group, Inc.
29 East 21st Street, New York, NY 10010

First Edition

Editor: Greg Roza
Book Design: Rachel Rising
Illustrator: Matías Lapegüe

Photo Credits: Cover, pp. 1, 3, 4, 6, 8, 10, 12, 14, 16, 18, 20, 22, 23, 24 Evgeniy Dzyuba/Shutterstock.com; pp. 6, 8, 10, 12, 14, 16, 18 (insert) Levent Konuk/Shutterstock.com; p. 7 AR Pictures/Shutterstock.com; p. 22 Greg da Silva/Shutterstock.com.

Cataloging-in-Publication Data

Names: Nagelhout, Ryan.
Title: The unofficial guide to building bridges in Minecraft / Ryan Nagelhout.
Description: New York : PowerKids Press, 2019. | Series: STEM projects in Minecraft | Includes index.
Identifiers: LCCN ISBN 9781538337042 (pbk.) | ISBN 9781538337035 (library bound) | ISBN 9781538337059 (6 pack)
Subjects: LCSH: Minecraft (Game)–Juvenile literature. | Minecraft (Video game)–Handbooks, manuals, etc.–Juvenile literature.
Classification: LCC GV1469.M55 K47 2019 | DDC 794.8–dc23

Manufactured in the United States of America

CPSIA Compliance Information: Batch #CS18PK: For Further Information contact Rosen Publishing, New York, New York at 1-800-237-9932

Contents

The Open World

Imagine a world where you can do anything you want. If you see a winding river in your way, you could move it or build a simple or fancy bridge so you can cross it with ease. If you've ever wanted to do something like that, *Minecraft* is the game for you.

Minecraft is a sandbox game, which means players can roam the game world at will, building structures and changing the land. The things you can do in the game are only limited by your imagination. You can also learn about engineering and **technology**. That will help you build amazing bridges in the game!

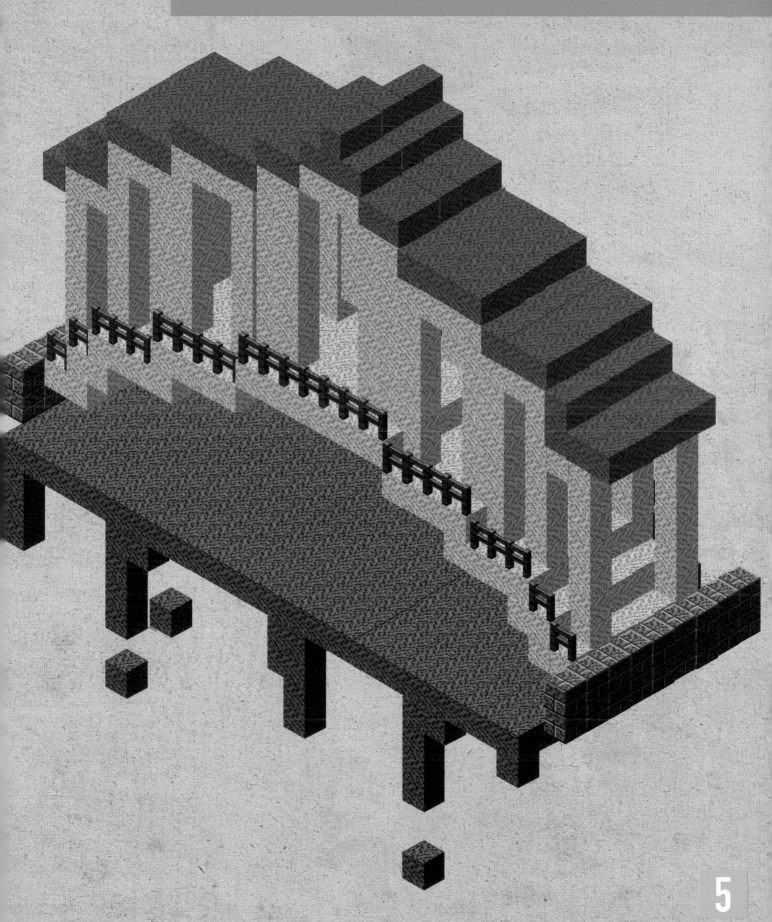

Minecraft is a game that lets you build just about anything. But many things you build in the game, like bridges, can be found in real life!

Real-Life Bridges

People have been making bridges in the real world for a long time. Bridges help people cross areas they can't walk or drive over. Some bridges cross bodies of water, such as lakes or rivers. Others go over other roadways or let things such as trains move overhead.

In *Minecraft*, bridges can help your character walk over dangerous things such as lava or canyons. You can **design** a railroad bridge that crosses an underground lava pit or a footbridge that connects mountaintops. You can build bridges out of many different **materials**, but finding the right kind can help you make the perfect bridge for your world.

MINECRAFT MANIA

Bridges in real life are made up of two main parts: supports that hold the bridge up and a **span** that crosses the road or body of water the bridge was built to go over.

Many things in *Minecraft* are made to replicate, or copy, things in the real world. Bridges are useful both in *Minecraft* and in real life!

Blocks and Gravity

Blocks are the most important building material in *Minecraft*, and there are many different kinds of blocks out there. Dirt, grass, and stone blocks are everywhere. Other kinds of blocks make up different things. *Minecraft* trees are made of blocks of leaves and wood. You can mine blocks of ore and other **resources** underground, then use these blocks to make new things with your crafting table.

Most blocks aren't affected by gravity, which means you can stack them in strange shapes and they won't fall. This makes it easier to build things, especially bridges!

MINECRAFT MANIA

There are different kinds of **modes** in *Minecraft*. In Creative mode, you get all kinds of different blocks to build with without having to search for them. Plus you can fly!

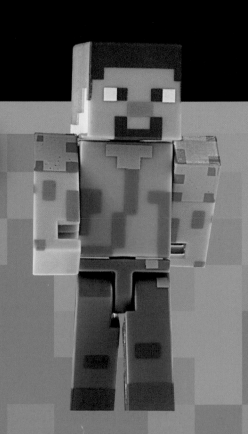

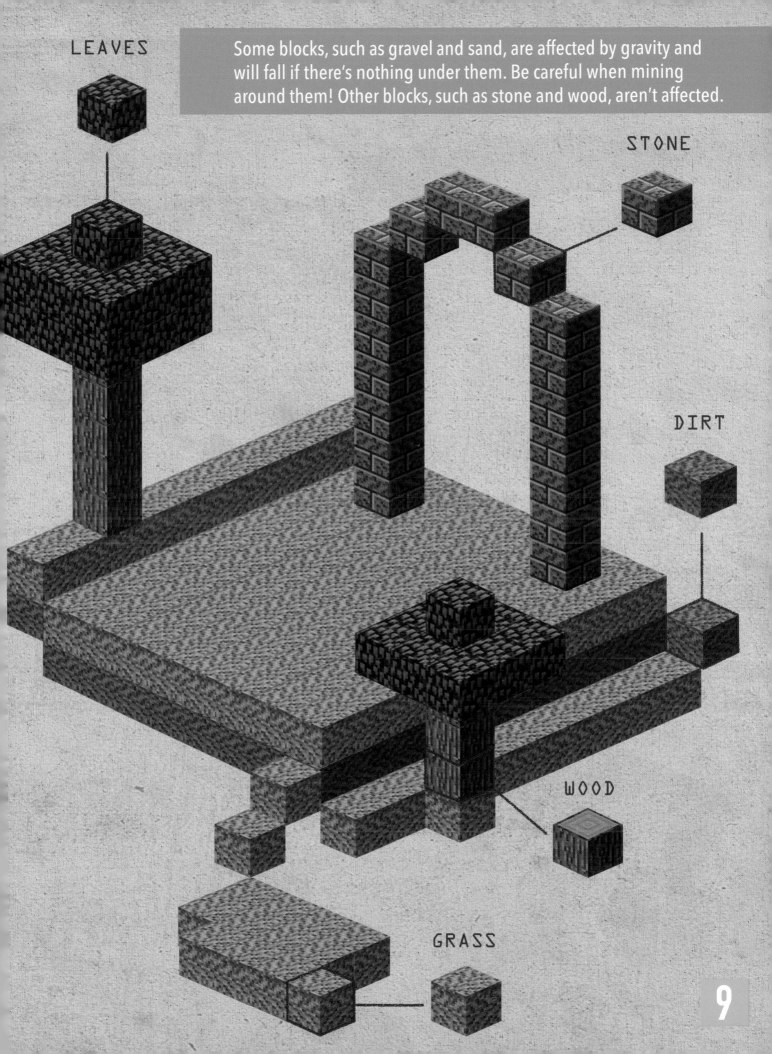

LEAVES

STONE

DIRT

WOOD

GRASS

9

Where to Build

Most bridges are built because they're needed to cross an **obstacle**. *Minecraft* has different kinds of obstacles, such as water, that can make it hard to travel. Building over water near your home can make it easier for you to get to other areas nearby.

You also might want to connect big hills together using a bridge or even build a bridge to go over a flow of lava. If you fall into lava, you can get hurt and even die and lose all your supplies. Use stone instead of wood when building near lava. You should always be careful near lava, especially if **mobs** are around!

MINECRAFT MANIA

Bridges in the real world need to be built to support a lot of weight. But in *Minecraft,* your bridges aren't affected by weight or gravity if you use the right kind of blocks.

Kinds of Bridges

Just because gravity doesn't impact most blocks in *Minecraft* doesn't mean you can't build a fancy real-world bridge. Your bridge can look like one of the many different kinds we have in the real world. An arch bridge has supports that arc up to the span to support its weight.

Other bridges, such as suspension bridges, have cables above the span to help suspend, or keep up, their weight. A beam bridge is the most common type of bridge. It's just a straight span over the water with supports underneath. This is the easiest type of bridge to build.

MINECRAFT MANIA

You can also build aqueducts in *Minecraft*. An aqueduct is a man-made channel constructed to move water from one place to another. For example, if you want water to build a farm in a desert, you could build an aqueduct to bring it to you.

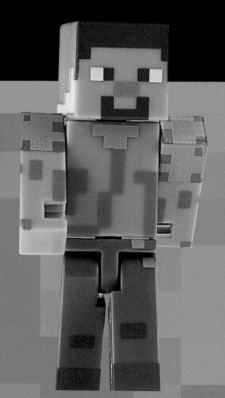

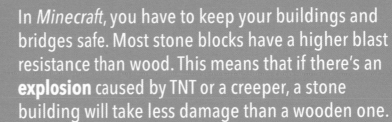

In *Minecraft*, you have to keep your buildings and bridges safe. Most stone blocks have a higher blast resistance than wood. This means that if there's an **explosion** caused by TNT or a creeper, a stone building will take less damage than a wooden one.

arch bridge

suspension bridge

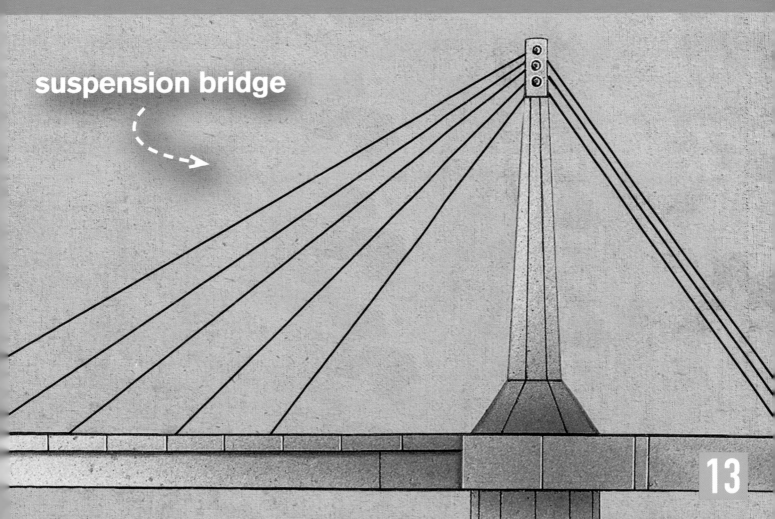

Start Small

Once you've chosen where you want to build your bridge and what material you want to build with, you can start building! Most times it's easiest to start with the span of your bridge. Start on the ground and build yourself some **scaffolding** so you can reach the area you want the span to cross.

One way to keep yourself from falling as you make the span of your bridge is to crouch as you build. That way you can see the end of the last block you set at your feet and add to it without falling!

MINECRAFT MANIA

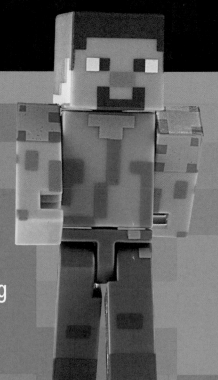

Scaffolding can keep you from falling too far if you're building high off the ground. If you fall in Survival mode, you can take damage or even be killed! You can always take down the blocks you use for scaffolding when the bridge is finished.

Wide And Tall

Simple bridges over short distances don't need to be fancy. They can be made from wood or dirt and simply connect two areas together with a flat span. But longer, more **complex** bridges can be more fun to build. You can use your simple, one-block-wide dirt bridge as a base to build a bigger bridge of stone or brick that looks like a real-life bridge.

Once you have a single-brick span, you can widen it on either side or make it taller by building above your span. Make sure the scale of your bridge matches the area around it!

MINECRAFT MANIA

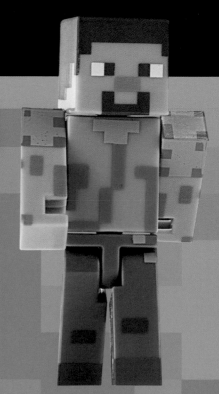

Making bridges that are symmetrical, or have the same amount of blocks on each side, can help the look of your project. Counting the number of blocks in a span and marking the middle with a special block can help you make sure your bridge is symmetrical.

Knowing where the middle of your bridge is can help you build arches that are symmetrical or help you build a tower in the center of your bridge. From there, you can keep it safe!

Bring the Obstacle to You

Minecraft is so fun because you can change almost everything about the world you play in. You can even bring the obstacles to you. Try building a bridge, then putting something underneath it, such as a pool of lava. If you want to build a castle and keep it safe, you can use bridges to help you do so. You could dig a moat, which is a deep, wide channel that runs around your castle. Build a bridge or two over the moat. If you have a bucket, you can fill the bucket with water or lava and then fill your moat.

MINECRAFT MANIA

If you have redstone and know how to use it, you could make a bridge with a span that moves up and down so it can only be used when you want. This is called a drawbridge!

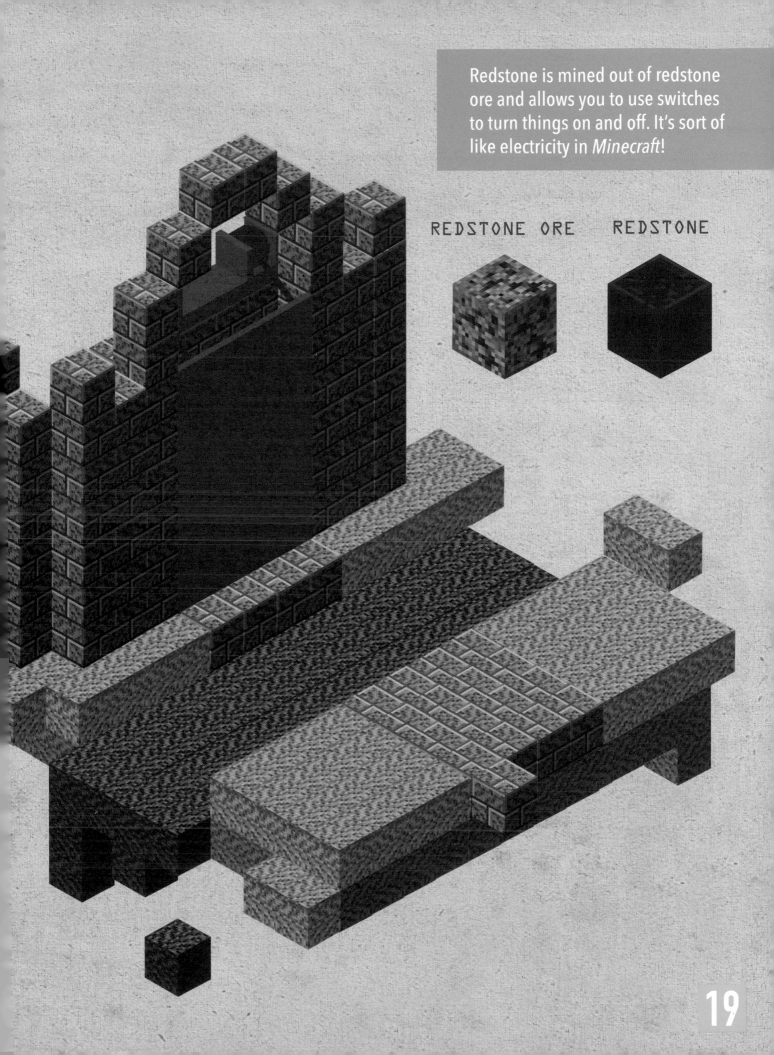

REDSTONE ORE   REDSTONE

Build Your Dreams!

Bridges are just part of the fun you can have with *Minecraft*. Even if you don't want to make a bridge a main feature of your world, knowing how to build one can help you get the resources you need.

See coal in some rocks overhead? Or gold ore near that lava flow? If you use the right blocks and safely build a bridge, you can get to the ore and mine it for yourself! Building bridges also teaches you about engineering, which can help you build many other amazing things in *Minecraft*.

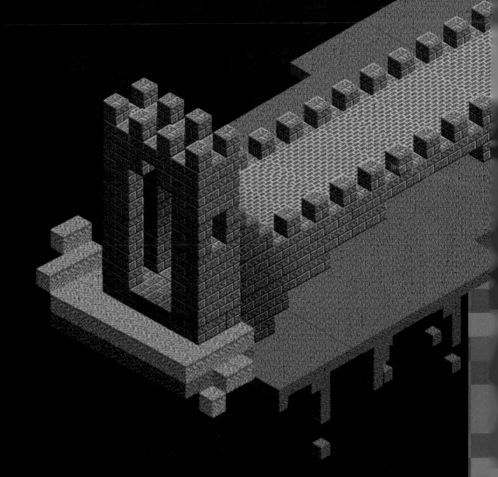

Knowing how to make usable bridges can change the way you play *Minecraft*!

Making Mods

You can make your *Minecraft* creations even more exciting with modifications, or mods. Using a computer program called ScriptCraft, you can create new blocks, change the way the game functions, and make your own games. Imagine what you could build! Maybe you could build a bridge of ice that never melts—and slide down the other side. Or you could build bridges among the clouds!

If you're interested in learning how to create mods in *Minecraft*, visit the website below. You'll find the information needed to get started with ScriptCraft and build your own *Minecraft* mods.

https://scriptcraftjs.org

Glossary

complex: Having many parts.

design: The pattern or shape of something. Also, to create the pattern or shape of something.

explosion: A sudden release of energy that causes harm.

material: Something from which something else can be made.

mob: A moving creature within *Minecraft*. Often used to mean one of the monsters that spawns, or appears, in *Minecraft* at night.

mode: A form of something that is different from other forms of the same thing.

obstacle: Something that makes it difficult to complete an action.

resource: Something that can be used.

scaffolding: A system of scaffolds, or raised platforms for workers to sit or stand on.

span: The part of a bridge that stretches over a length and is supported by the rest of the bridge

technology: A method that uses science to solve problems and the tools used to solve those problems.

Index

Websites

Due to the changing nature of Internet links, PowerKids Press has developed
an online list of websites related to the subject of this book. This site is
updated regularly. Please use this link to access the list:
www.powerkidlinks.com/stemmc/bridges